Healing Starts Here
This Time, I Choose Me

Written by Diosha Davis

To my beautiful daughter, Aryasia:

You are my world and the best thing that has ever happened to me. You are my friend, my peace, and my inspiration. Words aren't enough to express to you just how much I truly love you. You continue to encourage me to reach higher heights. You believed in me when I didn't even believe in myself and loved me when I was struggling to love myself.

God knew exactly what He was doing when He brought you into my life. He knew that I needed you, your love, your guidance, and your protection.

While working on this book, you'd come close the bedroom door and tell me that you didn't want to disturb me while I was writing. Periodically, you'd peak your head in just to give me some words of encouragement. I needed that.

You make your Mommy so proud! You're such a wise, kind hearted soul and as long as I have you in my life, I have everything that I need.

&

To those who are suffering in silence:

This book and journey is dedicated to you. I know how it feels to be afraid, so I want to be your voice. I want you to know that I see you and you too can get through whatever it is that you're going through. Although our journeys in life may not be the same, I believe that we all yearn for the same thing, satisfaction. We want to feel satisfied with who we are and the things that we have done in life. Fulfilment like this, makes us feel complete. No longer will I dwell in the darkness and allow my past to dictate who I am or who I am destined to become. And no longer should you suffer in silence because your *Healing Starts Here*.

Contents

Part II: Embracing My Truths

Healing Starts Here

Part I:

Unveiling My Truths

Introduction

I f the older me could talk to my younger self, I would tell myself how beautiful I was as a little girl. I would tell myself that my dark skin, kinky curly hair, and full lips were the traits of a goddess. I would tell myself that you could be anything in this world you aspire to be if you put your mind to it. I would tell myself that it's ok to be different. And even more importantly, I would tell 16-year-old me to fight back that night when those guys took advantage of me. I would tell 20-year-old me not to lose sight of myself in this cruel world. I would tell 25-year-old me to slow down, stop stressing, and working myself to death, to enjoy life. And I would tell 27-year-old me how valuable my life is and that I have so many reasons to live.

Breaking The Silence
When I finally made up in my mind that I was going to write this book, I was ready to let go of my past and talk about the things in life that were hindering me from reaching my full potential and restricting me from being the best version of myself. I knew that discussing these things would require me to reminisce on my past, taking myself mentally and emotionally to very moments that

reminded me of the exact hurt that I felt during that time. I would even challenge myself to visit places where traumatic things had happened to me. I was determined to embody every aspect of my life.

Life has taught me that healing begins when we let go of our past hurts and learn to forgive ourselves for our mistakes. Healing begins when we are no longer afraid to confront our fears. Although we are not the things that we've been through, it's those things that make us who we are today. So why are we afraid of our past? Why do we allow our past to have so much control over our lives? I truly believe that our past is only as powerful as we allow it to be.

Muzzled by my past, I had kept my pain all to myself for years. However, when keeping quiet wasn't working for me anymore, and I started to deteriorate from the things I was hiding inside, I knew it was time to break the silence. I was determined to get to the root of my pain and my brokenness. I needed to heal.

Healing forced me to embrace my truths because it required me to address those things that brought pain into my life, and that hindered me as an adult. Like many people, there were a lot of things in life, that as I grew older, I just wanted to void my memory of. I wanted to live my life as if some of these things had never happened. Life isn't that simple, though.

In a world full of fakers, some of us still admire the truth. We admire real people with real problems; people who aren't afraid to admit that they or their lives aren't perfect. So often, when people told stories about themselves, they would leave out the raw details. They'd leave out the parts of their lives that aren't necessarily pretty. But it's those very moments in our lives that make our journey so valuable. For sure, the depths of our stories aren't always gratifying. Sometimes life can get extremely ugly and difficult to embrace, but it's those parts of our journey that create such beautiful testimonies and stories. It's important for us to share our stories because someday your story can save somebody's life.

When my life needed saving, I found myself inspired by the many women whom I had encountered in my adulthood. These were always beautiful, successful women who on the surface seemed to have it all together, but their scars naked to the eyes told a different story. Their pasts were always captivating, and although our lives differed, there was one thing that we all seem to have in common: there was something or some things from the past that we had experienced, which seemed to be affecting us in our adulthood. Something was interfering with

13

us becoming the best versions of ourselves. Whether it was the fear of failure, lacking a particular life skill, or the memory of a traumatic experience, *we* were restricting ourselves from reaching our full potential.

Furthermore, I wholeheartedly believe that sometimes the trials we experience in life aren't always for us. At times, we go through these things because we are strong enough to endure it, but it is for us to use our story as a testimony to save another life.

I had picked up my pen and put it down hundreds of times trying to find the perfect words to say. I knew that writing this book would be a challenge, but the biggest challenge I would endure was putting myself in a position mentally to revisit some of the very moments in life that were everything but comforting. However, it would be those exact moments that I would use as a platform to redeem myself.

I hesitated to share my truths because I was still struggling with my past and present afflictions. *How could I be an inspiration to someone else when I was dealing with problems of my own?*

I had always been a strong person, but even the strongest people have a breaking point. I had come to a place in life where my past was weighing heavy on me, and I felt as if I was suffocating. Crying out for help, but no one could hear me.

My faith was always something I relied on, but depression has an odd way of consuming you. They say that your faith is tested in your darkest places through life, and this would prove itself to be true.

Hopefully, by sharing my story, I will inspire you to share yours. As you travel this journey with me, I pray that you too heal, find inner peace, and learn to make you a priority. The fact of the matter is, there's no such thing as a perfect story. I merely learned how to embrace my imperfections.

We'll dig deep as I unveil my truths and confront my past. I'll share the ugly and uncut parts of my life, discussing those topics that a lot of people are too afraid to disclose of.

This is my story:

"A single sentence spoken at the right time could change someone's life forever." **–Unknown**

Chapter 1

Broken Beauty

E very day I woke up, dressed well, took care of my daughter, worked a full-time job, and maintained a social life all while battling depression. For years I dressed up my exterior to mask how I was truly feeling on the inside.

I had mastered the art of masking my pain and manipulating my emotions over the years because I was never the type of person who wanted pity for the things I had been through. I was always willing to work twice as hard if I needed to, to accomplish my goals.

In addition to my eager work ethic, my wardrobe had become such a vital part of my life. I always dress well because I strongly believe that the way you dress and carry yourself affects your overall mood. I always felt that people shouldn't know what I was going through or what I had been through unless I decide to share it with them. So, my wardrobe mostly consisted of vibrant colors and extravagant patterns. Things that made me look lively, even if I was really dying on the inside.

However, beneath all of the glamor and the charming personality lie something more profound - brokenness.

For a long time, I suffered from depression and the truth is, I was struggling to acknowledge it. My internal conflict with me accepting it was bigger than the disorder itself.

I was so used to pretending that I was okay that I didn't even realize just how deeply I was sinking in my own depression. "I'm okay." *Isn't that what we're supposed to say when people ask you how you're doing?*

Sadly, depression was one thing that people never really talked about in my culture. A lot of times, just expressing that you were mentally unstable was frowned upon. I remember a few times being told to just go to church or toughen up when I would share how I was feeling or the things I was going through. Being an African American girl, and growing up in a single-mother household, I was raised to be strong, taught to endure anything that this cruel world threw at me. Because of the many adversities faced in life, some streaming from my early childhood, I was supposed to be *invincible*.

Commonly, people perceive mental disorders as a sign of weakness, but it takes a strong person to admit that they are struggling with a disorder and an even stronger one to seek the proper care that they need to overcome it. I always wanted to believe that I was bigger than what I was going through at that time, but when I found myself dwelling in the darkness, I lost sight of who I was. I had become so accustomed to functioning while depressed, working, being a mother, hanging with friends, and so much more that I just tolerated it for what it was.

It wasn't until 2017 that I started to dig a little deeper. I had gotten to a place in life that I had never been before – mentally. The harder I tried to press through my pain and move on from my past, the more overwhelmed I became.

From Dallas to H-Town

In 2017, I relocated to Houston after being offered a job opportunity. I was definitely on a wave of new beginnings. I had just purchased a new car, found a great neighborhood to reside in, and enrolled my daughter into a new school. The idea of all this change was so refreshing. But I would soon have my biggest breakdown in this new place I called home. My past would follow me, and unhealed wounds that I had only applied temporary bandages to would eventually bleed out.

So, what *really* made me make a sudden decision to pack up me and my daughter's bags and move to a new city? I mentioned the new job, but truly I needed an escape from my reality, and this opportunity was the gateway that allowed me to do just that. I was hoping that this year had some great things in store for me after having a rough previous year. I had just gotten out of a toxic relationship, I was forced to move out of my apartment after my boyfriend at the time had been shot several times in my complex, and I had gotten into a bad car accident on my daughter's birthday- my car was totaled as a result of the accident and a few days after later, I miscarried a child.

The miscarriage in itself had driven me into a sunken place. For days I wouldn't sleep or eat. I'd just lay in the bed all day with the windows covered, not knowing or caring the time of the day it was. There was just something about the loss of the child that had shattered my spirit, as I continued to blame my stress and mental instability as the cause of the miscarriage. During that time, a lot was going on in my life, and I was having a hard time coping.

With all of these events occurring one after the other, I had more than enough reasons to pack up our things and leave when that job opportunity presented itself. I wanted a fresh start after losing everything. I just wanted to forget the things that had happened and move on.

We didn't have any family or friends in Houston when we decided to relocate from the place that had been home for our entire lives. I had no idea what the future had in store for us, but I figured it had to be better than what I was dealing with at the time, so, we left. Honestly, I didn't think much about it. I just left. I had always been afraid of stepping out of my comfort zone when it came to relocating, and I knew that if I pondered on it for too long, I would probably change my mind and not go. The idea of moving away from home with my daughter always made me feel uneasy, but this time was different. Although deciding this made me feel courageous, I was really looking forward to putting some things behind me.

I was off to a great start and flourishing in my new position and atmosphere. For one of the first times in life, I remember actually being proud of myself for doing something great and facing my fears. However, that bright smile on my face soon turned into a frown when my mom's health took a turn for the worst back home, and problems with family surfaced. I was straddling myself trying to deal with the hardships back home, yet still try to stay focused, take care of my daughter and continue to perform efficiently at work. By now, I was contemplating if leaving home had been a good decision or not. My stress was at its peak as I tried to continue thriving in my new environment and reconcile with the things that were going on back home. As if this didn't already weigh heavy on me, Hurricane Harvey hit Houston that fall, making me feel even more uncertain about my decision to relocate.

As more challenges arose, I could feel my faith weakening. I was a manager, so dealing with peoples' problems was second nature; however, dealing with others' problems while trying to maintain my own was overwhelming at times. By now, my life had taken an unexpected turn, and moving to a new city alone with my daughter had only made matters more severe.

Drowning

Remember that past I talked about leaving behind? Well, it found me. Ironically, it snuck up on me like a thief in the night, stealing every ounce of joy I was holding on to at that time. Although I dressed well every day, there wasn't a piece of clothing or makeup that could conceal what I was feeling on the inside. Pieces of me that I thought I had put back together over the years were slowly falling apart. I was drowning - mentally, emotionally, and spiritually.

Crazy thing is, I was familiar with that unhappy place because I had been there before. But this time, I was undergoing my deepest depression ever, and I was too afraid to ask for help. I didn't even want to have the word depression associated with my name, let alone my job title. I wanted to believe that I could overcome the things I was going through and that this storm, too, would pass like every storm, right? However, this time when the depression came into my life, it made itself at home and got settled in.

I so vividly remember lying on my living room couch, writing a suicide letter to my daughter. I had gotten to a point where I was contemplating life or death. I remember the warm tears rolling down my cheeks and falling onto my notebook as I wrote this letter while, my daughter rested peacefully in the bedroom. She believed in me so much, but I felt as if I had let her down. She thought I was a superwoman, and for her, I always pretended to be until my world came crashing down around me.

That night, I went into the bedroom as she slept and kissed her on the cheek before moving forward with my fatal plan. What had brought me to this point? What had led up to the very moment where considering suicide was even an option?

Thoughts like these had crossed my mind before, but I never actually seen myself acting on them until now. I often believed that if I could eliminate myself, I could rid myself of the pain that was destroying me on the inside.

Drowning... That's how I felt, consumed by my inner thoughts and the way I had planned to take my life. I planned to submerge myself underwater in the garden tub of the small apartment home that my daughter and I shared, forcing myself to suffocate. I knew that when my daughter had awakened for the morning, my side of the bed would be empty, and she'd call out for me as she always did. But this time, I wouldn't respond. I wouldn't be in the kitchen cooking breakfast or on the balcony listening to music; I'd be laid lifeless in our bathroom tub.

I had attempted this once before, forcing myself underwater, restricting my flow of oxygen until I could feel my body shaking, struggling for air. Then quickly bringing my head to the surface, gasping for air.

However, that night in the living room after I prepared my letter, I took out the time to make a list consisting of reasons why I was giving up and a list of reasons why I should keep going. The comparison was twenty to one. That one was the only reason I could think of at that time why I wanted to live: that reason - my baby girl.

It was at that moment I realized that she needed me more than anything. I wasn't any good for her if I wasn't here. Although I had genuinely given up on myself, I hadn't given up on her. I was struggling internally, but I was determined to keep fighting for her. Giving up isn't an option when you have someone looking up to you, so a part of me wanted to give life another chance.

A few months later, while conducting chores around the house, I came across that suicide letter. I had hidden it in a safe place, knowing that these thoughts were still in the back of my mind.

I sat down and read the letter. I could feel the brokenness buried within me as I read the depths of my pain. Bothered by the things I was reading and reminded of the thoughts running through my mind that night I was planning to take my own life, I turned on my kitchen stove, set flames to that letter, and watched it burn into ashes on my balcony. I wanted to rid myself of everything I was feeling that night. I wanted to destroy the hideous things I had allowed to push me over the edge.

From that day on, I made a promise to myself that no matter how heavy life weighed on me, I wouldn't dare allow myself to even consider suicide an option ever again.

The truth is, at first, it hurts... then, it changes you.

Chapter 2
Domino Effect

If only it were a bad dream, I'd wake myself up a thousand times to escape the excruciating positions that I found myself in through life. People often experience traumatic situations in life that scar them, change them, and even end them. Circumstances like those had the power to turn a good girl bad, to force someone into the darkness forever, the power to drive suicidal and homicidal thoughts! I know all too well how it feels to be in that predicament, and it isn't pretty.

Good Night Gone Bad

It was a night like any other Saturday night. My friend and I were anticipating attending a house party that had been the big talk of the week. We always made it a point to show our faces at the athletes' parties or cool kids in school. We too had hosted a few parties ourselves in our teenage years. House parties were the "it" thing on the weekends back in the day. But this weekend would turn out to be a complete disaster, and the scarring it would leave behind would be eternal.

I had packed my bags and headed to my friend's house. She had talked her mom into taking us to the party, and we were looking forward to a night filled with fun. As nighttime fell, we got ourselves dressed and headed out. We were on the suburban side of town, outside of the neighborhood in which I grew up. I always enjoyed going on that side of town because the houses were massive, and the neighborhoods were beautiful. When her mom dropped us off at the party, the house was already packed, and the DJ played the hottest hits. We didn't hesitate to join the crowd and mingle with others. My friend and I didn't attend the same high school, so I wasn't really familiar with the other teens at the party, but that didn't stop me from interacting and having a good time.

A little while after the house got overly crowed, my friend suggested that we leave and go to another party hosted by some football players from her school. I was planning to stay overnight at her house, so I wasn't really worried about the time. She made a call to get us a ride to the party, and we made our way to the other side of town. Party hopping and catching rides with other teens was common during that time. We were all at that age where either you already had a driving permit or you were working on getting one, but if you had it, it was your responsibility to shuffle others around.

When we arrived at the complex and walked inside, there were only a few guys there. Two were familiar faces because I played sports, and we had crossed paths at a couple of events. They stated that the party hadn't started yet and that more people would begin to show up soon. We sat on the couch, listening to the music play as we waited. One of the guys made a suggestion to get more beverages, and he wanted to go to the store across the street. My friend decided to go with him while I stayed. She told me she'd be right back, and I didn't mind staying behind because she wasn't going far.

If I knew what would have happened next, I would have made a totally different decision. Moments after she left, one of the guys came and sat next to me. We were chatting at first, then he started to touch on my body, rubbing his hands aggressively on my legs, causing my dress to lift. I moved his hand several times, asking him to stop - which only seemed to aggravate him. He ignored me and continued to touch me. When I stood up to pull down my dress and go outside to wait on my friend, he grabbed me, pulled me down to the floor, and forced himself on me. I could feel him using the weight of his body to keep me in place as he pinned my hands to the floor, using his other hand to remove my underwear while I squirmed to break myself free.

I guess him holding me down wasn't enough, so his friend joined in to assist him in pinning me to the floor while he pulled out his penis and forced himself inside of me.

"Stop!"

"No!"

"Please!"

"Don't!"

All the words I uttered, begging them, hoping that they'd feel sorry enough for me to actually stop. But none of those words meant anything to them. Back and forward belligerently... I could feel him pushing himself inside of me as his sweat dripped onto my face. "If you scream, I'll hurt you," he told me as he picked me up and positioned my body in ways for his disgusting satisfaction. "Ya'll want in?" he asked his friends, who stood alongside watching me be abused and humiliated. His friends didn't hesitate to join in at his request.

Four of them and one of me.

I could feel my hair being pulled and multiple aggressive hands touching my body, as they all partook in forcing their penises into my vagina and mouth. Not even the sight of me gagging, choking, crying, and vomiting was enough for them to give in as they twisted and turned me into all types of uncomfortable positions.

At some point, I had given up. I had given up fighting and just laid there lifeless as the music played loudly in the background. I could feel myself fading away as tears rolled down my cheeks. You ever been so afraid that you don't even make a sound, you just lay there, slowly dying on the inside?

Eventually, they were done treating my body as their playground. I managed to curl myself into a fetal position with my underwear hanging loosely at my ankles, shivering my face covered in snot and tears.

Oddly, the bastards stopped when one shouted, "That's enough ya'll, leave her alone!" They adjusted their clothing, then picked me up to adjust mines. One wrapped his arms around me and told me that they were sorry; that they didn't mean for this to happen. Speechless and weak, I walked dreadfully towards the front door.

Where was my friend? And why hadn't she come back for me? Did she forget about me, or did she intentionally leave me there? I got on my phone to make a call, and one of the guys told me if I ever spoke about what had happened, he'd kill me.

Sadly, I believed him.

Since my friend was nowhere to be found, they offered to take me home. I guess that was their way of ensuring that I didn't see or speak to anyone else that night. That ride home was the longest ride ever. I could see the driver continuously turning his head, glancing at me in the back seat as I rested my head on the window, staring into the sky. All I wanted to do was get home and wash their filth off of me. I felt so dirty, so ashamed. *Why hadn't I fought back? How could I allow these guys to take advantage of me and me not even defend myself?*

When I arrived home, it was pretty late. I quietly entered our home in hopes of not waking my mom, showered, then curled in my bed under the covers. I could still feel the soreness in my vagina from them forcing themselves inside me and still smell the stench of their cologne on me after showering vigorously.

Why didn't I tell? I was afraid to. I didn't know who to tell, let alone how to tell. I had told myself a million times that I shouldn't have gone over there in the first place. I had convinced myself to believe that it was all my fault for putting myself in that situation.

It seems like one bad situation always leads to another... and another one. All until it's just one big domino effect. That painful night became the beginning of my domino effect.

What exactly is the domino effect? You finding yourself in a whirlpool of similar situations that you just can't seem to escape. It simply means that one catastrophic event triggered other negative things to happen.

After that incident, I found myself in many compromising situations with guys who wanted to be sexual, and when I refused, they would just force themselves on me anyway. I've had guys get verbally and physically aggressive, then at some point, I'd just give in. (This may be peculiar to some, but a person who's been there before "over stands" me).

Why is it that a girl or woman saying "NO" to sex codes as this ill yes in some guys head? Why is it that the aggressor somehow believes in his mind that his victim is enjoying this hostile activity? The idea of it all just turns my stomach.

Being taken advantage of repeatedly was one of those things that had led to my brokenness and one of those things that had started to consume me later in life as a woman. At times, I would look in the mirror and be so angry with myself. The reflection I saw was a weak woman who didn't take up for herself and who had allowed people to hurt her. I hated myself for being so vulnerable at some points in my life.

I never wanted my daughter to experience the same type of hurt I experienced. And when I started trying to get to the root of my brokenness, it was circumstances like those that I knew I had to address for my own healing. It's brokenness like that, that spills into our adulthood - affecting us mentally and emotionally in our lives, relationships, careers, and so much more.

The little girl in me was hurting, and over the years, all I had done was bury that hurt with more hurt and glamourized the exterior in hopes that I could cover how I was truly feeling on the inside. Covering our pain with glossy lips and glittered eye shadow doesn't mend us, though. Just as your make-up cracks when the foundation isn't laid properly, so do we. The slightest crack in a foundation can cause the entire structure to fall apart. My structure was falling apart because over the years, all I had done was continue to build onto an unstable foundation, never really addressing the real issue.

Although this incident happened to me as a young girl, I still found myself bearing that hurt as a woman. If you never truly heal the broken little girl in you, she'll continue to dwell within you, searching for fixings that make her feel fulfilled, even if those fixings are hurting her.

Chapter 3
Seventeen & Pregnant

I had met this guy in high school during my sophomore year, who at that time was one of the sweetest persons I had ever encountered, and I fell for him. He would carry my books for me while he walked me to class, always had my back, opened doors for me, and was always so patient and gentle with me. He wasn't like a lot of guys I had met in high school. He never forced himself on me and wouldn't even kiss me without my permission. For a teenager, he sure knew how to make a girl feel special.

Loving him was easy because he always had my best interests at heart and his circumstances with his parents at that time only drew me closer to him. I wanted to be there for him anyway I could and show him that people loved and cared about him. However, somehow, letting him go was easier than loving him. After we both decided to partake in sexual activities, I found out I was pregnant, and that's when EVERYTHING changed. He began slacking off, skipping school, and for a while, I was unable to reach him.

My career as a high school athlete had been put on the back burner and my hopes of getting an athletic scholarship started to feel unrealistic. I was unable to finish my track season due to the pregnancy and had started working my first full-time job to help support the baby. I wasn't making much back then, but it was something to help me establish a little responsibility as a soon to be teenage mom.

Breaking The News

Statistic shows that most teenage pregnancies are amongst Hispanic and African American females, in which about 30% of those pregnancies result in a drop out of high school.

I had already become a part of statistics by becoming pregnant at seventeen, but I refused to allow these statistics to dictate my life. I had always been an honor roll student and ranked at the top percentile of my class throughout my high school years. Although there were a lot of teenage moms and pregnancies in the high school that I attended, I never found myself parading around. In fact, being seventeen and pregnant made me feel uneasy. I wasn't ready for what would come with that lifestyle. I had already let my mom down, and at that time, I felt so bad for the attention and shame I had cast on her life.

Telling my mom about the pregnancy was tough. After finding out I was pregnant at the clinic on campus, and visiting a church clinic for a second reading, it took me a couple of weeks before I even shared the news with her. I knew how much of a letdown this was going to be for her after all the hard work she had put into being a single parent, and even more, I knew that this would just be another burden on her because I definitely wasn't fully capable of caring for a child at that time.

When I told her about the pregnancy, I wrote her a letter and placed it under her pillow. I couldn't even fathom the thought of standing face to face with her and telling her not only that I was sexually active but that I was pregnant too! The night I left her the note, I was a nervous wreck. I sat on the living room couch with the TV muted and could hear her unraveling the letter. By now, I was sweating, thinking to myself *she's going to kill me.* When I heard her footsteps coming down the hall, I knew this was it! "She's coming to knock me out!" I said to myself. When she made it to the living room and stood in front of me, there was a moment of silence while we locked eyes with one another. My mother was the type of person who rarely had to peep a single word to my sister or me; there was just something about her demeanor that spoke volume.

When she began to speak, one thing I know, and two things are for sure - she was angry, but more importantly disappointed. It's one thing to upset your parents, for me, my mom. But it's a real disclaimer when you disappoint them. I never wanted to disappoint my mom and when I did, that was a load that weighed super heavy on me.

Just the idea of the position I had put her and our household in saddened me. I'm not going to lie. I was ashamed. I would wear looser shirts when out and while at school. I hid my pregnancy outside of my home until I could no longer conceal my protruding belly. I wanted to do everything I could to not draw additional attention to my mom.

I had always been a vibrant kid, but during that pregnancy, I stopped being as interactive and social as I usually was and spent a lot of time by myself. Being a child and being pregnant was nothing to flaunt about, in my opinion.

Struggling To Keep Up
I gave birth to my daughter during the fall of my senior year. I was doing my best to keep up with my school assignments while on pregnancy leave, but those late nights, early mornings, and trying to keep up with the baby were definitely wearing down on me physically and mentally. I

was tired, stressed, and overwhelmed because being a young mom was hard. This was one of those things in life that I had not planned for, not at that age anyway.

Not only was I swamped with assignments from my teachers while on leave, but when I arrived back to school that winter, the track season had already begun, and I was so far behind. I had run track ever since I was seven years old, and when I got to high school, my goal was to earn a track scholarship.

But all of my years of hard work went down the drain when I found myself struggling on the field to get back in shape after giving birth to my daughter. Having a baby takes a magnificent toll on a woman's body. I was no longer one of the elite athletes in the school, and my dreams of going to any of the top colleges for track were fading away.

After entering the track season extremely late and failing to make a comeback in my track career, I quit in the middle of the season and decided to solely focus on my academics. Although things didn't pan out exactly as expected, I was offered a full-time academic scholarship in the spring of my senior year.

This was exactly what I needed after my track season had plummeted. This reward was bittersweet, though. I didn't want to go to a university that was far because I had my daughter at home, and my mom and I decided that if I attended a college within the city limits that I should still stay on campus to focus on my education, so I did. I enrolled at the University of Texas in Arlington and began attending school that fall. I would stay on campus during the week and come home on the weekends to be with my daughter.

Being away from my daughter during the week sucked, and I started indulging in a variety of activities to occupy my time. Sometimes that free reign in college is a pathway to pure destruction.

Consequences Of Bad Decisions
While at school, I started getting myself involved with some negative things and my academics began to slip. I managed to recover my grades that first semester, but after falling behind again during the second semester, I was removed from the scholarship program.

The being out late nights, missing classes, and turning in assignments late had caught up to me. When my scholarship was taken away from me, I took it pretty hard. Education had always been a priority of mines. I was always an honor roll student and always in the top percentile of my classes. So when I lost that scholarship, I lost my mind along with it. People can take anything from you, but they can't take what you know.

Getting full-time scholarships weren't the type of opportunities that people got where I came from. To have received something so significant and lose it behind poor decision making, I was devastated and found myself in a very dark place in life.

If losing my scholarship wasn't enough, I found out at the end of my second semester that my bad decision-making had really caught up to me this time! I made some decisions that weren't always the greatest as a teenager, heck we all have, but this particular decision would cost me and change my life forever!

Chapter 4
Letter To My Unborn

For three months you grew inside of me.

I still wonder if I hadn't made that decision, how you'd be.

Would you have a smile like mines, would your curls be loose or tight?

Damn! What was I thinking, paying these people to take your life!

At times I wish I never did what I did.

I got rid of the sonogram pics, thought I could void all memories of it.

I sit back and think how I knew you would have been great.

How dare I take your life and have the audacity to call it a mistake!

But I was only 19 years old, how was I going to care for two kids?

I still beat myself up about it, wish I would have never done it.
I lay in my bed and shed tears, wishing I could go back to that day.

I was your mother, I was supposed to give you life, not take it away.

This was a poem that I wrote after deciding to have an abortion. I titled it *"Letter To My Unborn"* because I wrote it to them one night when I found myself crying, deep in my feelings, and I wanted to apologize for what I had done. I was having some regrets about my decision after it was over and done.

I was always taught to use my words to express how I was feeling, and poetry always allowed me to do that. Although my life went on after that day, I would always find myself thinking about what I had done, and my feeling of rue followed me.

A Feeling Too Familiar

During the spring of my 2nd semester in college and after feeling ill for a few days, my roommates suggested that I take a pregnancy test. I didn't think that I would be in that predicament again, but those bad decisions had definitely caught up to me.

Here I was, nineteen years old, at the end of my first year in college, I had a one-year-old, I was unemployed at the time and had recently been notified that my academic scholarship was being taken away from me. Stressed was an understatement.

When I found out about the pregnancy, I felt Seventeen and Pregnant all over again. I knew that this would come as a great deal of disappointment to my mother. How in the heck was I on baby number two when I couldn't even solely provide for baby number one?

I knew that there was no possible way that I could put my mother in a compromising position again, trying to help me care for another child, and the thought of the embarrassment that this would bring to her was eating me alive.

My family was always so judgmental and never missed an opportunity to gossip about someone else and their circumstances. I didn't want that for my mom. I had always made it a priority to protect my mom's image, even if mine was ruined in the process.

Mind Made Up
The day when I decided to go to that abortion clinic, my heart was so heavy. Although I had so

many reasons why I had made this decision, none of them were particularly for me. So many times in my life, I found myself making decisions based on someone else and not always necessarily for myself. Or I found myself making decisions based on someone else's expectations of me. I had it bad always putting others' thoughts and feelings before my own. Anyway, when we arrived at the clinic, I waited in the car for a while before even entering the building. My college roommates were there to accompany me. When I walked into the clinic, the waiting room was full of teenage girls, like myself and some way younger than me. But we were all there for the same reason. It was so quiet, and there wasn't a single smile in the room.

Upon checking in, I was advised on how the procedure would take place and the cost. Remember when I said that this decision would really cost me? Well, it did- literally! I didn't have a dime in my pocket that day. The clerk at the clinic told me that I could potentially qualify for some financial assistance but that I would need to cover the rest out of pocket. Back in the car, we got on our phones, making numerous phone calls to agencies who supported abortions and seeing if friends would allow us to borrow money to cover the cost.

After getting everything that we needed on the same day, the procedure was scheduled. I remember lying on the operating table in the freezing room while the nurses prepared my anesthesia. It wasn't my first time undergoing surgery, but this time was different. This time a life was being terminated as a result of it. They had already done the sonogram, told me how far along I was, and sat me with the counselor before moving forward to see if I wanted to change my mind.

I remember speaking with the counselor and not really saying much. I just listened, never asked any questions. I just wanted to get this over with and move on with my life.

Secrets Surface
My life never truly moved on after that. That abortion was one of those things that stayed with me throughout my life as a young woman. On many occasions, I would just find myself crying in my bed at night for the decision I had made. I felt selfish for giving birth to one child and killing another. I would feel so disgusted with myself for allowing all of this to happen. As years went by and life went on, that part of my past followed me everywhere.

When I had packed up my bags and moved to a new city, that abortion was one of the memories I was hoping to also leave behind. But that night in the living room, when I prepared that suicide letter, I was reminded of the things that had brought me to this point. The things in life that had weighed so heavy on me. Secrets that I thought I buried were all surfacing and haunting me like a bad dream.

It was mishaps like that in life that had made me feel like a terrible person. How dare I just move on with my life knowing the awful things I had done?

The crazy thing is that a year after that abortion, my life took a dramatic turn for the worst, and I began spiraling downhill fast...

Chapter 5
Addicted

After having a hard time getting back enrolled in school and working a minimum wage job, I was more than frustrated with my circumstances. I was barely making enough money to care for myself, let alone my daughter, and I was still living at my mom's house because I couldn't afford to live on my own. Being a mother and not solely providing for my child made me feel a certain type of way; it made me feel worthless. I needed to establish some independence for myself and find a way to provide for both of us, so I reverted to some things I had started getting involved with in college.

Money Is The Motive
Back in college, I had gotten introduced to exotic dancing. Initially, it was just a way to make some fast cash and put a little money in my pockets here and there to cover small expenses. I had promised myself that I wouldn't get too deeply involved because I already had some challenges academically, and that wasn't the lifestyle that I was trying to live. But, when my life wasn't going as planned, and that minimum wage job wasn't

cutting it, I started dancing full-time. I worked rotating shifts as a cashier at the grocery store, so I would dance on my days off and before or after my shift.

I started convincing myself that school was really just a waste of time, and while I was sitting in long classes getting lectures, I could be out here making money in just a few hours. Yet, dancing for fun or because you want to versus dancing because now you have bills to pay, a child to feed, and a roof to keep over your head is totally different. It changes the game. When I started dancing in school, I didn't necessarily have any major responsibilities. My schooling was covered by my scholarship, my daughter was with my mom, and I received government assistance for her at the time.

However, when I decided not to return to school and move out, dancing became a part of my life. It became my full-time job. Making the money was easy, but the lifestyle that came with dancing was a different type of monster. The type of monster that you don't hear about as a child.

Not Myself
When I found myself deeper in the lifestyle, I could see and feel how it took a toll on me mentally and physically, but by now, I was already so deep. I wasn't concerned with how it

was affecting me. I was addicted. I was addicted to the lifestyle and what it was doing for me financially. I was able to go to the mall and buy me and my daughter whatever we wanted. I could take her anywhere she wanted to go, and money wasn't something we lacked at the time.

It wasn't the addiction to the lifestyle that was killing me, though; it was the alcohol and drug abuse that was devouring me. It was just something about the strip club, something about the men staring at every inch of your body as you worked the stage, something about the way they would touch on you, putting their hands in places where they didn't belong. It was just something about taking off your top for the whole world to see everything except for the small bit of your vagina that your G-string covered. It was the only thing that was slightly hidden; everything else was on display for the world to see. For me, dancing sober was never an option. Stripping was something Diosha couldn't do. The alcohol and drugs allowed me to be someone else. Whenever I was under the influence, I was not myself.

Although the drugs and alcohol clouded my vision of my reality in the strip club, it didn't change my reality in the real world. A lot of times, women liked to glamourize the dancer lifestyle, but no one really talks about the things that go on behind the scenes or what truly comes with it. Everyone praises you on the stage, but truly, that's a rough lifestyle to live. I was always watching my back because of the hours I was out, and I definitely got myself involved with a lot of cold-hearted people during that time.

As a dancer, most of the relationships that you involve yourself in are about the money. You too become so cold-hearted because you can't afford to have yourself or your feelings invested in a lifestyle like that. Everything is temporary, and if you aren't focused, you can lose the money as quickly as you earned it.

Lost

Plenty of nights, I can recall stumbling up the stairs into my home after working at the club. Although I was involved in that lifestyle, I was always thankful for the grace and mercy that God had over my life. Him always allowing me to get from point A to B in one piece. It's crazy because I loved going to church. It was just something about the word that gave me strength and hope even though my life had spiraled out of control. After working late on a Saturday night into the morning, it wasn't uncommon for me to go home, shower, take a nap, and go to church on Sunday mornings. Sometimes I would still be hungover from the night before, but that didn't stop me from serving a God that had been so good to me. His word was always nurturing to my soul. It may sound odd to some, but even when you go astray, those things that are of value still manifest within you.

However, when you choose to indulge in a certain lifestyle, you are susceptible to everything that comes with it. And when you choose to partake in certain activities, you are open to the consequences that come with it as well. So often, people want God to do these miraculous things in their life and want Him to swoop down and save them from all of their troubles and bad decisions, but it doesn't work like that. You are giving free liberty to make your own decisions even if they cost you big time.

And because I chose to indulge in that lifestyle, I felt the aftermath of my decision-making full throttle. I had been robbed before, had things stolen from me and my home. I've had things put in my drink, been abused, taken advantage of, and so much more.

But there was one thing that would change my life forever. The one thing that I had said I would never do was the exact thing that saved me from my path of destruction.

Overdosed
It was a night like any other. I showed up at the club, freshened up, got dressed, and ordered my

drinks before hitting the stage. My preference at the time? Anything that would get me intoxicated enough to forget about me stripping in front of hundreds of people. That particular day had been a long day already. I was tired, the late nights were wearing down on me physically, and my daughter was heavy on my mind. After being in that world for so long, I started thinking about so many women who had not made it home one night because of the life they chose to live. *What if that was me someday?*

Anyway, a lot was going on in my head, and I couldn't seem to focus, so I ordered more drinks.

When the DJ got to my name, I asked him to skip me because I wasn't ready. My mind was all over the place, so I asked one of the dancers if she knew anyone was selling pills in the club that night. I just really wanted to get out of my head, get on stage, and make my money for the night. Dealers were always in the club, and although I was not big on popping pills, I had done so a few times while working in the club. After making a purchase and taking the pills, my night began.

Things were going quite well that night. The club was packed, there were some big shots in the building, and there was a lot of money to be made. I remember while dancing, I was started to get dizzy, and I was sweating heavier than usual. When my vision started getting blurry, and I could feel myself blacking in and out, I knew it was time for me to wrap it up and call it a night. I went to the back, got dressed, and called for someone to come pick me up. I was feeling too weak to drive. By the time my ride arrived, I didn't even have the strength to walk myself out of the club, so they came inside and carried me out.

"Is she okay?" I could hear people asking as my body lay slumped while they carried me out of the club. By now, everything was fading in and out. One minute I was here and could hear people speaking to me in the car; the next minute, it was nothing, just darkness, and silence. "Diosha, nod your head if you can hear me." I nodded slightly to let them know I was still conscious.

"Take her to the hospital," someone said.

"No, we don't want her mom to see her like this."

Then again, there was nothing, just darkness. I remember waking up to the car stalled, people crying, calling my name, and telling me to wake up. I could see the reflection of red and blue lights on the window. "I think she's okay," someone said as I stared confused about the commotion going on around me.

"Your eyes rolled to the back of your head, and you stopped breathing… we thought you were dead."

I had overdosed and was unconscious for a while.

Having people tell me that made me feel uneasy about the lifestyle I was living. It's hard to imagine that I had blacked out to the point that I don't remember anything. It's scary knowing that at some point in your life, you stopped breathing. I read too many stories about people dying from overdoses, but this time again, the Lord had spared me. That particular situation made me reconsider my entire outlook on how I was living. Something had to change.

That's Enough

I had always made it a point to make time for my daughter when I lived that lifestyle, even after the late nights and early mornings. I always made her my priority. It was like I was living a double life. During the day, we would go to the park, arcades, movies, out eating, everything. And at night, I would take her over to my mom's and head to the club. I never wanted her to know the things I was getting myself involved in after hours, so I kept those two worlds separate. I remember when she was three years old and only stood at the height of my lower thigh, she would always hug my legs, look up at me and tell me that she wanted to be just like me when she grew up.

But who was I? Who had I even become?

I was at the point where I barely recognized myself, and I surely wasn't the amazing person my daughter thought I was.

How did I get here after always being at the top of my classes, being a big-time athlete, and receiving multiple awards due to my academics and athleticism- one award being that full-time academic scholarship? How did I go from all of this greatness to stripping at a night club?

I didn't know who I had become or how I had got to this point, but I knew it was time for me to make a change. Although change isn't always comforting, I was willing to do whatever it took to get my life back on track and to be everything that my daughter believed that I was.

Chapter 6
At War With Myself

A fter the overdose incident, I didn't go to work for a few days. I just sat at home, re-evaluating myself and my life. Then one day, I finally got up, went to the strip club where I worked, and cleaned out my locker.

I didn't really know what was going to be my next move after that. I just knew that the life I was living at the time wasn't going to cut it. The day I cleaned out my locker, I remember the other dancers asking where I was going and telling me that I'd be back. "They always come back," I could hear them saying as I exited the club doors.

Never Looking Back
I never looked back, though. In fact, from that moment forward, I made a promise to myself that no matter how complicated life had gotten, never go back to stripping. The same day I cleared out my locker, I got on the internet and starting reading about the Army. I searched for a recruiting center near me and scheduled an appointment.

When I arrived at the office to meet the recruiter, before I entered the building, I just sat in my car watching soldiers pass by. It was just something about their walk and the way they carried themselves. While I waited in the car, I sat there contemplating whether joining the Army was a good idea or not. However, I was in desperate need of a change in scenery. I needed to do something different to get my life back on track.

When I finally found the courage to go in, I remember everyone staring at me in a bizarre way as I made my way to the recruiting offices. I guess I didn't look much like army material then. No one in my family had gone to the army, so I didn't know anything about it or what I was really getting myself into, but I eventually found out.

I enlisted soon after that. Making the sacrifice to join the Army was one hell of a decision. Although I knew this decision could change my life and open doors, the thought of leaving my daughter behind was stressful.

People joined the military for different reasons, but I didn't go for the schooling, benefits, career opportunities, or because I was patriotic. I didn't enlist because I wanted to go to war, even though I knew that was a possibility. I enlisted because I was at war with myself. I was fighting for my life. I was fighting for my daughter. I was fighting for our future. I knew that if I continued to engage in my old ways, I would only be headed down a path of destruction. I wanted to be a better version of myself. I knew that woman that I someday wanted to become needed to be strong enough for my daughter to lean on.

Mental & Physical Training

The Army had an interesting way of molding you. Their way was intense but rather satisfying because the training that you undergo doesn't only prepare you for war; it prepares you for life. The military helped saved my life in a sense. So many times in that street life, I had managed to dodge death. The tragedy that I had witnessed people lose their lives from, I had survived and was granted the opportunity to live another day.

The Army tested my body and mind in dynamic ways, pushing me to limits that I didn't even know existed in me. Only the strong survive. From camping in harsh weather conditions, walking miles until my feet bled, gas chambers, combative training, intense obstacle courses, and so much more - you were pushed far beyond your limits. So many times, I wanted to give up, but I couldn't. After long days when I would shower, I would allow the water to run on my face to conceal the tears falling from my eyes.

Training was tough but being away from my daughter tore me apart. I wasn't able to see her or hear her voice for months. Although I was missing my baby girl, I continued to remind myself of why I had made this decision in the first place. This sacrifice was for us. Sometimes in life, we are forced to make sudden decisions that hurt but can potentially change our circumstances.

Returning Home
I was looking forward to returning home. I couldn't wait to get back to my daughter and pick up where we had left off. This time would be different for us. I had gained so much in my time spent training and was ready to put some of those things into perspective.

When I returned home, I spent a couple of months enjoying the company of my family before I decided to get back into the workforce. I also decided to put my schooling on the back burner. At the time, one of my priorities was being able to financially provide for my daughter and sitting in classes for long periods of the day wasn't going to pay the bills, put food on the table, or a roof over our head.

I worked a couple of dead-end jobs before landing a position in management. Working a full-time job was a challenge, though. I found myself frustrated with the scheduling and the "waiting to get paid every two weeks" thing. Being a dancer allowed you to work your own hours, and there was always money to be made. You don't have to necessarily wait on it. I had worked a few jobs prior to dancing, but after you taste that lifestyle, your expectations change. I continued to find myself at war within - knowing what I needed but yearning for the things I wanted.

I wanted to be able to solely provide for my daughter and me. I wanted to make money, but I just wanted to make it differently this time. "The streets aren't the only way to eat," I would always tell myself. Yet, so many times, I would find myself having to postpone bills or skip events because I was waiting to "get paid." I was recreating myself, though, trying to teach myself discipline and patience.

When my finances would get tight, I would think to myself that one night of dancing couldn't hurt, right? But the thought of one of my employees coming into the strip club and seeing me performing on stage made me reconsider it every time. I had created a reputation for myself based on the life I had been living, and I was doing my best to change it. Even though I had left that lifestyle behind, the world is small, and there were some employees who were familiar with my past.

The Battles Continue
The more I tried to thrive in my role as a manager, the more I felt uneasy about what people knew about me. A lot of times because of my past, I would feel like I didn't belong in Corporate America. My background differed so much from the other managers. I always tried to dress and carry myself in a manner that didn't remind me so much of the person I used to be and the life that I had lived in the past, but I would always feel like people could see straight through me.

That move to Houston was such a fresh start for me. It allowed me to come into a new environment where people didn't know me or know of me. When I relocated to Houston, I also transitioned to a new unit to continue my military training. The military had opened so many doors for me and had helped put me in a position to take care of my daughter like I always wanted to.

Although my military contract ended in May of 2019, the real war continued. The war within self - me wanting to better myself, wanting to heal, wanting to experience true peace and happiness was ongoing. Those were my constant battles, and just because you've gained a victory in a battle or two doesn't necessarily mean that you've won the war.

Chapter 7
Daddy's Little Girl

S peaking of ongoing battles, one of the battles that I always found myself conflicted with was the one involving the role that my father played in my life - or the role that he *didn't* play in my life. Honestly, I'm not sure which is more sufficient. I am sure that all of the things that he did or didn't do somehow still affected me as a woman.

Even though I had gotten older and started to live my own life as a young woman, I started realizing just how much certain things had affected my life and led up to some of my unhappiness and brokenness. Now I am not the person who blames others for the mishaps in my life or blames people for my own lack or failures, but this hurt was different.

I had started feeling a lot of emptiness later in my life. Although I had my daughter with me, I was working a pretty decent job, and things were going copasetic; there was just this void that no relationship, money, opportunity, or materialistic object could fill. My heart was feeling so heavy years succeeding my last break up, and although I had moved on from that relationship, I just couldn't figure out why I was feeling so empty inside. After going through several depressions, some more severe than others, I was determined to get to the root of my brokenness.

Have you ever had your heart broken before? I'm not referring to that particular hurt you feel after a bad break up. I'm talking about a *real* heartbreak. That heartbreak that scars and changes you. If so, do you remember who caused you that pain?

I thought I had experienced heartbreak before until I realized who the first person was who truly broke my heart. And the first person who had ultimately broken my heart as a young girl was my father.

The lack of the role that my father had played in my life had done significant damage and was still affecting me as a woman. In my late 20's, here I was longing for his attention, for his time, for his guidance, and his love and affection. It wasn't enough to just say "I love you" only through text messages - I needed and wanted to know what it sincerely felt like to have his love expressed to me.

But why now?

As a child, I had grown accustomed to his part-time presence in my life, so I couldn't understand why now, as a woman, I wanted to have him there. I guess I wanted so bad for him to be the one that I could have called when my feelings were hurt, to be the one I called when I had been let down, for him to have been the one I called that night when those guys took advantage of me... I wish I could have laid in his arms when I felt alone or afraid and have him wipe the tears from my eyes. I wanted to know what it felt like to be Daddy's Little Girl.

I wondered how much of a difference in me it would have made if he were there to pick me up off of the ground when I fell from my bike, to kiss me and tell me everything would be okay. Would it have made a difference if he were there to have my back when people hurt me? What if for every time I felt afraid, I could call on him? Maybe those nights of me sleeping with a chair propped behind my front door or nights with a knife next to my bed wouldn't have existed because I could've called on him to feel protected.

Protected - a feeling that I longed for. I wanted to feel safe. I wanted to feel secure.

I always wanted my daughter to feel protected whether, she was with me or not, to know that I was only a phone call away. The role of being a parent is never truly done, no matter how old your children get. Well, at least for me, I want my daughter to feel like she can always come to me, talk to me, and express herself to me as long as she needs to. And I know the role that I'm playing in her life will determine whether she feels comfortable or confident enough to do so, even in her adulthood.

The Importance of Roles

Roles were important in our lives, in our development, in our relationships, and so much more. But in order to know your role, I think that we needed great role models to follow and look up to. When it came to roles, I definitely fell short throughout my role as a woman in a man's life. I was one hell of a mother, but dating and relationships didn't seem to be my strength.

I had grown up in a single-parent household with my sister, led by my mom. Yes, a house with only women, so when it came to things such as mowing the yard, cutting bushes, fixing the plumbing system, taking out the trash, fixing minor car malfunctions, and so much more - those were all things that we took care of. There wasn't a man around to take care of every single task that was needed. So indeed, my mom instilled the teachings of "taking care of your own and not depending on anyone" in me.

And although I turned out quite independent and have my own everything, that still didn't stop me from wishing that I had someone that could take a bit of the load off of my shoulders and wishing I had someone who could genuinely love me and not love the things that I did for them. That is exactly where I went wrong. I was always doing - always giving.

I was always giving so much of myself to people who didn't deserve it, specifically men. Knowing the things that I lacked, I always made it a priority to give so much to others so that they never felt as if they too were lacking. I would give this limitless love in hopes that I would get it in return, in hopes that my empty voids would soon feel filled.

However, the only thing I was doing was adding to my hurt by having expectations for people to heal a heart that they didn't break. And having expectations for men to play a role in my life that I, myself, wasn't even familiar with. Heck, what was a man's role in my life, anyway?

I didn't really understand a man's role in my life or my role in theirs because I was never really given a decent example of that. My mom taught me how to take care of my business and to take care of people. So I lived my life always ensuring that others were taken care of, and putting other people and their problems before myself and my own. I clung on to a lot of people, some of which were hurting me, but my desire for a certain type of love was deep.

It was evident that after the breakups and failed relationships that this emptiness that I possessed wasn't meant to be filled by just any man, but the man who had given birth to me.

During my early 20's my father and I tried rekindling our relationship, but years later and after some family issues arose, I was left with a bitter taste in my mouth about him all over again. I think, at times, he struggled with owning his faults and had so many excuses as to why he fell short instead of just trying to do better.

I think we all have dealt with some things in life that may interfere with us becoming the best versions of ourselves; however, I believe it's important that we put in the initiative to do better, and when we don't, that's when we fall short as parents.

Having expectations for people always leads to disappointments, though. I guess I just expected him to try a little harder. I expected him to know how important his presence would have made in my life. I expected him to know that his little girl needed him - even still as a woman.

My dad had already broken my heart as a little girl, and here I was as a woman still operating in that same hurt, still having that animosity towards him for missing so much of my life and being angry at him for not being there for me when I needed him the most. Was he too wrapped up in himself to realize the heartbreak that he had caused?

Not Her Too
I did my best for things to be different. I didn't want the same hurt for my daughter, but the day when she sat me down and asked me why her father didn't love her, I knew I had let her down. Although my daughter's father did not play his role in her life, I never spoke negatively about him. I actually thought that if I could give her every ounce of the love that I had to offer that maybe she wouldn't notice his absence. You can't miss something you never had, right? She associated my love for her with me always being present in her life, caring for her, and doing the things that I did for her. He was never there, though.

No matter how hard I tried to distract her with my love, she noticed something, well someone was still missing. I remember when she was only about two years old, she drew this picture of this little family. She pointed at the picture and told me that it was a baby, a mommy, and a daddy. She told me that this was how a family was supposed to look. For the first time, I told her that families were always different and that even though it was just her and I, we were still a family.

Although I did my best to provide a beautiful life for her. That still didn't stop her from inquiring about her dad and his lack of presence in her life. For years I had made up excuses for him to prevent her feelings from being hurt until one day, she asked me to just tell her the truth about him. But could she handle the truth? Could she handle the fact that her father just failed to play his role in her life for his own personal reasons? Could she handle the heartbreak that she doesn't even know she's going to experience in life because of it?

I never wanted that type of hurt for her and was willing to do everything in my power to prevent it. But there are just some things in life that you cannot intercept as parents, and there is just some hurt that you cannot protect your children from.

Hopefully, I've Done Enough

The day she asked me about her dad, she cried...
I, too, found myself crying, reflecting on my hurt
and brokenness stemming from my father. I
couldn't force her father to be in her life, but what
I could do was reassure her that I would always
be there.

I could never understand how a father
didn't play a role in his children's lives, especially
daughters. Girls were so easily engulfed by this
cruel world. Although I was tough, the role of a
father is one I could never fill. How could you not
want to be her protector? How could you not
want to be the shoulder's that she cried on? How
could you not want to be there teaching her,
leading her, and loving her?

I had so many questions as a woman,
knowing that someday the role that my
daughter's dad did and didn't play in her life
would eventually affect her, just as it did me. I
wondered if she too would find herself later in life
feeling empty inside, yearning for her dad's love
and affection. I hoped that she didn't find herself
in my shoes though, clinging to men, longing for
them to fix a heart that they didn't break because
this only led to more heartache and was a
centerpiece to my brokenness.

Chapter 8
The "Perfect" Kiss

Dear Daughter,

In the midst of my triumphs and failures, I remember that you are my motivation, strength, and push to work harder. When life seems to bring me down and I feel like I have no one to turn to, I turn to you. I am going to make life easier and better for us one day. I love you with all of my heart.

Love,
Mommy

A lot of times in life things don't go as planned, however sometimes it is those exact unplanned circumstances that change our lives for the better. Giving birth to my daughter was like that. I knew eventually in life that I wanted kids, but I never thought that I'd find myself pregnant and giving birth to my first kid at seventeen. A situation at the time that was one of the most embarrassing, fearful, and disappointing points in my life, turned out to be one of my biggest blessings.

At first, I couldn't imagine how my life was going to be when my daughter came into it, now I can't imagine my life without her in it.

Sometimes we'll spend a lifetime searching for something that's been in front of us the entire time. For so long I was searching for a love that was forgiving, a love that was limitless, reassuring, and healing. I wanted a love that wasn't contingent upon the things that I did or didn't do, but that was unconditional. It was love like this that mended broken hearts and helped put us back together again.

Keep Me Close

I spent so much of my time clinging to things and people who were breaking me, and you were there to put me back together each and every time. There were nights when I would just lay in your small arms and cry while you held me tightly, wiping the tears from my eyes. How could someone so small, so young be so wise, so passionate, and so angelic? An angel in disguise. That's exactly what you are for me.

When life took a toll on me, it was you by my side, holding my hand the entire way. When I said that I couldn't, you said that I could. You believed in me when I didn't even believe in myself and you loved me when I was struggling to love myself. You watched me grow from a girl to a woman and I am everything that I am today because of the love you've given me.

You are always so gentle with me, knowing exactly what to say and when to say it every time. You have no idea just how much you are changing my life.

You Saved My Life

My life is far from perfect but there was one thing about it that was perfect for me in each and every way - my baby girl. It's just something about the way she holds me, kisses me, and loves me that changes me; making me a better woman, mother, daughter and so much more.

That night in the living room, when I was contemplating suicide - it was her who saved me. I had so many reasons why I wanted to give up and she was the only reason why I just couldn't give in. After all the things I have been through, and after all of the loses and downfalls, she makes it all worth it. Never missing an opportunity to tell me that I am doing a great job and always reminding me how much she loves and appreciates me.

I need her. She is my lifeline. Even though, I had gotten to a place in my life where I was ready to give up on myself, I wasn't ready to give up on her.

I knew a young woman once who was getting abused by her boyfriend. She came to me in tears, asking me what she was supposed to do. She told me that she had given up on herself long ago and would rather be dead instead of undergoing the abuse. She had two children and told me that if she wasn't here, her children wouldn't have to see her go through that. Although she had given up on herself (something I was all too familiar with because I had been there before), I told her that she had to fight through it, that she couldn't give up on her babies because they needed her. Just as my daughter needed me.

She is the most important thing to me. She means more to me than life itself and I was willing to do anything to pull myself out of that dark place to be there for her.

Sometimes as adults, we get so caught up in the things going on around us in life that we forget to just live. We forget just how beautiful life is and spend a lot of time stressing, rather than making the best of the things that we already have and the people whom we have to share them with.

The one thing I admire most about my daughter, is her ability to teach me and open my mind and heart to things that I wasn't used to. She is always so affectionate, which was odd because that wasn't something that I was used to. She is always kissing on me, holding on to me and wanting to be under me. I've always appreciated her language of love, although it was not one I was too familiar with. It is different and it makes me feel different. It is like that little piece of something special that I have been missing my entire life.

Teaching Me A Different Way

I remember when my daughter used to fall or hurt herself while playing and I would always just say, "get up, you're okay, you're a big girl, or don't cry" but when I would get hurt, she would always come running to my rescue, get down on her little knees and kiss me where it hurt. She would be so patient and so gentle with me, so nurturing and I started realizing that she needed that too from me.

I was a sensitive person, but I never really showed certain emotions until I started observing her, watching the way she handled and cared for me. She was teaching me, teaching me to be more affectionate and patient.

In addition to all of these things, she was teaching me to just live. For years, I had spent my life stressing about work, finances, relationships, everything, and she would always tell me to be thankful and proud of the things I had and that I was doing.

One day, I told her that someday I wanted to be able to buy us a home and she replied saying "that our place was a home because her and I were there together; that no matter where we went, as long as we were together, it would always be a home." It was words like that from her that always made things so much better.

I struggled with being a parent when I had my daughter at first. I was young and had absolutely no idea what I was doing. I didn't feel like a mother at times because of my circumstances and due to the way my life was going, but she was always so proud of me, no matter what I was doing.

I was always beating myself up and feeling like I had failed in so many areas in life, but to her I was always a winner. She was my biggest fan, my biggest supporter, and my rock through it all. Her believing in me alone, taught me to never give up.

Her random kisses and text messages are so refreshing to my soul. "I'll never be too old to kiss my mom," she always tells me. Although I wasn't accustomed to that type of affection, I always tell her to keep loving her mommy the way that she does because it is changing me, healing me, and making me a better person.

Because of Her

Although I held onto a lot of hurt for years, I never wanted my brokenness to spill over into my daughter's life. And when the burdens of my past started overwhelming me, getting the best of me, and interfering with our relationship, I was determined to heal.

I remember there would be days when I would come home, and she would ask me to play and I would be too tired. Stress had started getting the best of me. The things around me were draining me and my quality of life was fading. I didn't want it to be like that anymore, so I gained back control of my life.

In order for me to be any good for my daughter, I needed to be good within myself. I wanted to be the best mother I could possibly be for her and I was willing to do anything to do just that.

I would always thank God for putting her in my life. It was because of her that I had grown so much and needless to say, it was because of her why I'm still alive today. Sometimes in life we have to find something, even if it's just one thing that inspires us and pushes us to keep going even when we don't necessarily feel like it. My daughter is my "thing". She gives me so many reasons to get back up every time I get knocked down.

I wrote her the letter above when I was nineteen, before she could even speak or read because someday I wanted to be able to express to her just how much she means to me. Now here she is sending me text messages routinely to express to me just how much I mean to her.

Know that you are good enough.
Please don't give up when things get tough.
I know it hurts.
Just know that you do have worth.
You are my light in the dark.
You will always have the key to my heart.
I love you more than you will ever know.
Promise me you won't let go.

Love,
Daughter

Part II:

Embracing My Truths

Chapter 9
Don't Be Afraid To Protect Your Peace

So, when does healing truly begin? I said earlier in the book that healing begins when we let go of our past hurt and learn to forgive ourselves for our mistakes. Healing begins when we are no longer afraid to not only confront our past but embrace it for what it is. Would you be the person that you are today if it wasn't for the things you've been through? I know sometimes that's a hard pill to swallow because our past isn't always the most pleasant. There were a lot of things in my life that, as I grew older, I just wanted to move on from. I wanted to live my life as if these things had never taken place. We have to realize that those things don't necessarily just go away, though. They don't disappear just because you've moved to a new city or because you choose to change your life and/or the people in it. They are part of us, part of our journey, and part of our truths. And either you accept those parts about you and your story, or it consumes you.

Healing is an individual task. It starts within self. For such a long time, I believed that someday this "great guy" was going to come into my life, help me pick up the broken pieces, and make everything all better. But that isn't my story, and I don't believe that's how healing actually works. I'm no expert or anything, but it's safe to say that even when I was involved with someone, I would put a lot of my focus into that person, rather than myself. I think we all have a tendency to put our problems aside when we are focusing on other things. No one wants to necessarily feel like they are baggage in a relationship. Sometimes we'll subconsciously put our problem down and pick up someone else's without even realizing it. This isn't just in regard to companionships but also relationships with family and friends. How many times have you actually disregarded yourself or what you had going on to be there for someone else? I've done it several times myself. I was so used to helping and being there for others that I was neglecting me. I was forgetting that I too needed that same time and attention that I was investing in others. I needed to make me a priority.

Forgive me if this sounds ruthless, but I had to learn that sometimes I needed to ignore calls and texts from people that I loved to 1) make me a priority and 2) to protect my peace. Peace is something that, during my healing process, I realized was one of the most important things for me to protect. People will disturb your peace if you allow them to. Sometimes you don't realize how critical something is to you until it starts affecting your well-being or your mental state. When I was on the road of recovery, it was critical that I was able to recognize those people or things that were interfering with my peace and healing. Here's a harsh reality for you - sometimes the people hindering you the most are the ones you love most. Ouch! I know that hurts, but it's true. We all have that friend or that family member that calls with drama or who only reaches out to you when they need something. I don't know about you, but that is extremely draining!

What about those people that you are always pouring into? Encouraging them, giving them advice, being their personal counselor, and they never stop to even just ask, "How are you doing or how was your day?" People can be so inconsiderate at times. I knew people who would without any hesitation dump their entire load of problems on you and expect you to provide them with some type of gratification to make them feel better. And if you're anything like me, you're always trying to be there for others, be a shoulder for them to cry on and a listening ear - even if it meant setting self aside to do so.

There were so many things going on in my life when I was trying to heal that I could never truly focus solely on me. There was the stress of my job, my schedule, my finances, me being a single parent, my health, family problems, and so much more! Me, I tend to function better when I have control. By control, I mean being able to make certain decisions about the things going on around me and being able to somewhat dictate how I actually felt about those things, but I had to realize that I couldn't control all of these things. In fact, me trying to control everything around me only stressed me out even more. I realized that I needed to let go of some things.

One of my biggest stress factors was my job. I had worked in management for years. However, your expertise at the job is irrelevant with it comes to the importance of having a balance between your work and personal life. I was investing so much of myself into my employer and never really taking out the time to take care of me. Five days a week, ten plus hours a day, I was addressing everyone else's concerns, providing resolutions to their problems, and making myself professionally and emotionally available for their needs. I always felt like as a manager, there were some unwritten tasks that I was responsible for that weren't necessarily written in my job description. I was always so empathetic to my employees' needs that it started to drain me. I had this open-door policy where I allowed my employees to come and talk to me about any and everything. They definitely didn't hesitate to bring in their massive loads and to dump them right on me. So often, when I would leave work, I'd take their burdens with me, worrying about them, concerned if I had done enough, wondering if there was anything else I could do. This alone was fuel to my already existing depression that I was struggling to manage at that time and was doing everything in my power to suppress it.

One day, I said to myself, "That's enough!" I needed to control some of those things I was taking in and making myself responsible for when it wasn't actually my job to do so. I couldn't exactly control what these people were going through, but I could control how I chose to react and addressed the situations. I stopped making myself so readily available for the things that didn't involve actual work. I did away with a lot of the personal inquiries and started focusing on just being a manager and not a personal counselor. This, in itself, allowed me to protect my peace. Sometimes we can take in all this information that does nothing but weigh heavily on us mentally, emotionally, and spiritually. With that being said, I knew that if I had any chance of coping with the things that I was going through at the time, I needed to separate my work and my personal life and create a barrier around my peace of mind.

The Breakthrough

I think one of the biggest misconceptions about healing is that people believe that when you do begin to heal or have already healed from the burdens of your past that all of a sudden, their lives are perfect and stress-free from that point on. That isn't necessarily the case, though. In the spring of 2019, I started seeking counseling to help me understand and cope with my depression. In order for me to even get to this very important part of my life, I first had to admit that I had a problem because I was in denial for quite some time. I was so used to being the strong one, and I didn't want to believe that I had allowed myself to get to such a dark place in my life. Anyway, although the suicidal thoughts had gone away, the depression still lingered and interfered with my life. I was struggling with sleeping at night and was all too familiar with going into my zombie modes (times when I would just sit or lay around and do absolutely nothing - no talking, eating, watching TV, interacting, or anything; just lifeless).

When I decided to attend counseling, I had become so frustrated with how much my depression had taken advantage of my life and even more how it interrupted my parenting and relationship with my daughter. I had always been a vibrant person, but when depression started getting the best of me, gradually, I found myself less active, cooped up in the house more, and in a strict routine of just going to work, coming home and lying around. I was always fatigued and just physically and mentally drained, even if I had not done anything or been anywhere. It sucked because prior to me getting to this point in my life- my daughter and I would always hang out and play together. But the deeper I fell into depression, the more and more I faded away, losing sight of myself and the things that I enjoyed doing.

Counseling was a huge milestone in my life and was the beginning of a massive breakthrough for my healing. Even though I relied heavily on prayer and my spiritual beliefs, I believed that professional help was necessary for my recovery. When I first started attending counseling, I would do so secretly. I would tell my daughter I was attending a class because she always had a tendency to worry about me, and I didn't want my burdens weighing on her. I didn't want her to know how much I was going through at the time. My daughter was always a bright girl and eventually figured out that those evenings when I would grab my notebook and head out, that I wasn't going to any classes. I don't know if she had seen my notes from counseling, or something in my journal but she knew. When she decided to bring it up to me, she told me that it was ok and that she would be there to support me the entire way. That meant a lot. She had always been my biggest supporter, and having her be there with me through this process was exactly what I needed.

Counseling was intense, though. I liked the idea of sharing my life with this complete stranger who wasn't there to judge me but help me overcome the challenges that I was facing. It wasn't easy though, her bringing down my walls or her breaking through molds of hurt that had manifested so deep within me. There was one session that was the hardest of them all. We had gotten on the topic of my childhood and some of the things I had experienced. I had previously shared with her in another session that no matter how hard I tried moving forward in my life, it was like there was just this brokenness within me that I couldn't seem to fix. She was determined to get to the root of this pain that had been hindering me for such a long time now. I remember when I began to cry in her office one day, I hurried to dry my eyes and apologized for crying. Showing my true emotions in front of people was something that I had strayed away from the last few years. I felt like people took advantage of situations or people when you exhibited any sign of weakness. I could remember plenty of times in life where I had allowed myself to be transparent with my emotions, and people used those vulnerable moments to hurt me.

As she continued digging into my childhood, I couldn't help but remember that night at that party when those guys had taken advantage of me. She wanted to hear more about it, but the more I explained, the more uncomfortable I became. I avoided saying certain words and kept reverting to blaming myself rather than the guys who had partaken in this devious act. When she asked me what I would call what happened to me that night, I begin explaining the circumstances of the situation again. She stopped me and asked me again what those guys had done to me. I knew what she wanted me to say, yet I was struggling to call the act by its name. RAPE. It was just something about the word in its entirety that made me feel so uneasy and vulnerable. It made me feel naked, in a figurative sense, as if people could see through me. But the way people saw things and their perspectives were always complex. How many times have women accused a man of raping them, and they're being the ones blamed for dressing a certain way that provoked men or being the one persecuted for not fighting back. How many times had women been raped and a man justified it by saying that "Well, she didn't say no." At the age of sixteen, I myself had already known so many girls who had been victims of their step-dads, uncles, cousins, brothers, coaches, and so many more. Here I was just another victim afraid to speak up because I knew no one would believe me.

It wasn't until that counseling session that I realized that my problem was way bigger than just the act itself. I, too, had an issue with seeing things for what they were. It always made me feel a little better to see things the way I wanted to; that way I could avoid the harsh reality. If I could continue to blame myself for being at the party and blame myself for allowing something like this to happen to me then maybe, just maybe, I could force myself to believe it was all my fault and accept full responsibility. Then it probably wouldn't hurt so badly, you know. That was the victimized mind in me. That was the way I had trained myself to think from sixteen up to me being a woman.

Did you notice that I never said the word "rape" in Chapter 2? Remember, healing is an indefinite process. Although, I've accepted what happened to me that night. I still struggle with the act in itself. Sadly, that wasn't the first or the last time that I had been touched inappropriately or forced into sexual acts against my own will. I think it's easier for me to acknowledge that one because at that time, it included people that I didn't necessarily know. That may have gone over some people's heads, but I guarantee you a victim of sexual abuse caught that. Yes, sometimes it was those people that we knew and loved who had inflicted this pain upon us. No is no, right? The same rules still applied no matter who it was, but I think a lot of us had a hard time accepting that. Even more, I think we were afraid to accuse people that we love of raping us or taking advantage of us.

I'm speaking to my victims when I say this: how many times have you said, "No", and still been forced to engage in sexual activities? How many times have you gave up fighting back and just took it? How many times have you told someone that you've been raped and no one believed you?

I don't know if I've made my point just yet, but what I do know is that so many times, so many women had been through the exact same thing and had a tendency to react all the same; afraid, ashamed, disgusted, and unworthy. You don't speak up because, in your mind, you already believe that no one will believe you, but I do, and I understand exactly what you're going through.

Counseling taught me that it is okay to be vulnerable and that vulnerability isn't a sign of weakness but a sign of strength, proving that not only are we strong enough to have endured this pain, but we are even stronger when we choose to seek the help that we need to confront past hurts.

Acceptance At Its Finest

It was important we not only learned to accept our truths but that we had learned to love ourselves wholeheartedly. Sometimes we accept the things that have happened to us in life, but yet we still view ourselves indifferently or considerate ourselves insufficient because of them.

What do you see when you look in the mirror?

For a long time, when I stared back at myself in the mirror, all I could see was an ex-stripper who abused drugs and alcohol, who lacked a college education. All I could see was the poor decision making that I had made over the years, and to me, I thought that I'd never truly be good enough. After my last relationship, I realized that I loved everyone except for the one person that I needed to love the most - myself. I had a hard time loving myself because, in my eyes, I wasn't anything but a screw-up.

Loving myself first came with accepting and forgiving myself for the things that had happened in my life. Furthermore, loving myself came with me no longer allowing myself to just be an option, but a priority. This was tough, though. It's hard making yourself a priority when you are a parent and even harder when you're so used to caring for everybody else, but something as simple as saying, "This time I choose me," could change your life forever. It definitely changed mines. By choosing me, I was able to radiate happiness within myself that had been dulled by all of the things in life that were consuming me. By choosing me, I was able to preserve peace. After battling and recovering from severe depression, I had made a promise to myself to choose me, and with that promise, I was willing to lose anybody before losing myself ever again - this included family, friends, coworkers, etc. I was willing to cut all ties with anything or anybody that was interfering with my peace and happiness. You have to get aggressive about protecting yourself, wanting the best for you, and not be afraid to let go.

One of the biggest obstacles I struggled with when I embarked on this journey of acceptance was me accepting where I was in life at that time financially. I would always criticize myself for the decisions I had made in life and blamed them for my lacking. I would tell myself that if it wasn't for my terrible decision making that I'd have my own house by now with a yard for my daughter to play in, that I would have been married, or would have had this amazing paying job if I would have finished school. However, loving myself came with embracing every piece of me and my journey. The truth is, I was exactly where I was supposed to be in life. I wouldn't be where I am today if it wasn't for that journey. Too often, we compared ourselves to others and their successes when we are all on different paths in life. Timing is everything. See, I actually started writing this book about four years ago. Can you believe that? However, can you imagine how much of my life has changed since then and how much I've grown? I was nowhere near where I am today, four years ago. That's why timing is so important. Sometimes we get impatient and want to see the fruit of our labor immediately, but things that are so profound to our well-being take nurturing.

There are some seeds that you planted years ago, have fostered with tears, and the roots are just now starting to break through the ground. One of my favorite sermons is about how seeds are placed alone beneath the ground in the darkness to grow. We are like those seeds in a sense; sometimes we too need to be separated from everything and everybody to grow. Some of the most beautiful flowers began their development in the darkness.

That was me. It wasn't until I moved to a new city that I started to experience growth in ways that I never knew possible. Being away from everything and everybody forced me into a lot of things, but most importantly, being away made me realize just how strong I truly was. Sometimes you don't know how strong you truly are until you have no choice but to be.

I was able to uncover those strengths when I started believing in myself. For years I was notorious for putting myself down and beating myself up about the things I had been through. But let me tell you, when I let go of that hurt because that's all it truly is, I became a different type of force! There comes a point in your life where in order for you to get to your next destination, you're going to have to let go of some things and leave some things behind. Sometimes the only thing standing between you and reaching your full potential is you.

This Chapter Is About Me

So this isn't actually a chapter in the book. It's a chapter in my life titled, *Me*. *Me* is about all things that make me beautiful, resilient, strong, and worthy. *Me* is about getting out of the way of self to discover and create the best version of myself possible. *Me* is about overcoming and letting go of all the things that have hindered me in life. *Me* is about HEALING.

Our lives are really just compiled of mini journeys about ourselves that create divine stories, and we are the authors. You may not have gotten an opportunity to decide how that story began, but you definitely have full control over how you chose to end it. Will you use your story as a testimony to save another life, or will you learn from it, grow, heal, and lock it away in a special place for keepsake? Either way is amazing because everyone's healing journey is different. Some may choose to share, and some may choose to celebrate their overcoming in private. For me, writing this book and sharing my story *is* part of my healing. Yes, I said *is* instead of *was*. That's because loving and learning self is a never-ending journey. You always have to leave room for self-improvement in your life story. If not, how could you ever truly become the best version of yourself?

I know you're probably wondering, *what's life like for Diosha now?* Well although I've bounced back from depression and have learned to cope with the things going on around me (without any self-medicating, something that I'm extremely proud of myself for), my life didn't all of a sudden get spectacular from that point on. Hardships and trails didn't disappear. In fact, in the fall of 2019, I was notified by my doctor that I had a tumor on my brain. Now, knowing the old me, news like this would have sent me spiraling down the dark hole of depression, but it didn't. I'm not saying that I took the news well either. In fact, hearing it was catastrophic. It was the last thing that I ever suspected, and it took me down quite a bit emotionally. I actually took off work for a few days because the news was so overwhelming. However, the only difference between the old me who suffered from depression and this version of myself, is that I learned that when things get heavy and hectic in my life, that it is okay for me to pause for a minute to reset myself and realign my thoughts and feelings. I've learned that it is okay for me to be sad, it's okay for me to be angry and that it is okay for me to be confused. What isn't okay, is for me to find myself drowning in those emotions and allowing them to take over my life. I've too learned to get up when I get knocked down and to be more optimistic about the things going on around me.

There are so many things great going on around us, but sometimes we focus so much on the negativity that it drowns out everything else. We then tend to forget about those things that are going well in our lives. For instance, even though I was diagnosed with that brain tumor, it wasn't in an alarming state where I needed immediate surgery or anything. In fact, the doctor thought it would be a good idea to just monitor it, rather than prescribe me medication for it. That in itself was a blessing. Here I was with this tumor but yet my health was still great and I was in a substantial place in my life mentally, emotionally, spiritually and financially. A lot of things were going well around me and I wanted to emphasize more on those rather than soak in sorrow about something that could have potentially been there my whole life and it was just being brought to the light because of some inclusive blood work. I had too many things to be happy about in my life at that time so I didn't want to invest too much of my energy into that or I would be right back where I started from battling depression. I was reminded of how easy it was to get swallowed up in my own anxiety, usually by worrying about things for too long.

We have to learn that celebrating little wins or those things that are going well in our lives can make the difference. When was the last time that you actually told yourself you were proud of you? Or told yourself how amazing and beautiful you are? I didn't use to do that often, but now I'm always searching for an opportunity to compliment myself and pat myself on the back for accomplishments, even if it's small.

In this chapter titled *Me*, I've learned to stop stressing so much, to live life to the fullest and relax. I, too, learned to stop comparing my circumstances to others because everyone's journey is different. No you may not have this extraordinary home, luxury car, or perfect family because I surely don't, but the things that I do have are mines. I've worked hard for them and I'm able to share them with someone who means the world to me - my baby girl. It's so easy to get wrapped up in what everyone else is doing. You look at your age and start feeling like you are behind, when truly you are exactly where you need to be on your journey. Stop listening to other people tell you how you should or shouldn't be living your life, and just be you. Be you and embrace everything about you. Embrace that past because it has made you stronger but it doesn't define you. Embrace those intense life lessons that you've grown so much because of and embrace that brokenness because you can heal.

In this chapter titled *Me*, I learn the importance of investing in self. I was always so wrapped up in work. I was allowing my work to dictate my entire life. I would go to that job and pour every ounce of myself into it. Then when I got home I'd be so tired from putting my all into a company that would replace me in a heartbeat. I was pouring so much of myself into a company that could care less about my mental state, as long as I was producing. So I started taking that same time and energy that I was investing in that company and started investing it in myself. I started investing it in my crafts, and things that I actually loved doing that were important to me, like this book.

In this chapter titled *Me*, most importantly I've learned that "No one can make me feel inadequate about the things I've learned to accept, love and appreciate about myself." Once I mastered what it truly meant to forgive myself, nothing or no one was capable of making me feel "less than." I am done hindering myself by allowing negative thoughts to accumulate in my mind. I am worthy and deserving of everything I've worked hard for and so are you. So erase those limitations that you've created on yourself; thinking that you don't deserve an amazing paying job because you didn't finish college, thinking that you don't deserve to experience true love because of your past, or thinking that you don't deserve a happy family because you come from a broken one.

Name a perfect person with a perfect story.

I'll wait…

Furthermore, in this chapter titled Me, I've learned to forgive the people who have hurt me and those who have let me down. This forgiveness isn't for them; it's for me. I've learned that holding on to hurt only weighs me down and prevents me from moving forward. Some people may never be aware of the pain that they've caused you in life, but I had to realize that I couldn't change people. The only thing I can change is me and how I choose to live my life in spite of the things I've been through. I've forgiven those guys who took advantage of me that night at the party, not because they deserve it but because I deserve to live my life not haunted by the ugliness of my past. Most importantly though, I've forgiven me. I've forgiven me for the areas in life where I've inflicted pain on myself. It isn't until you've forgiven yourself that you'll experience true healing.

I forgive myself for the decisions I've made in life. It was those decisions that caused me to lose sight of myself. I forgive myself for being afraid of giving birth to another child and getting an abortion. I forgive myself for living a life full of addictions. I forgive myself for leaving my daughter for the Army in hopes of giving us a fresh start. I forgive myself for overworking myself then beating myself up for not being where I thought I should be in life. And I forgive myself for wanting to commit suicide.

Then I didn't know just how valuable my life was at that time, but I do now.

That day when I set flames to that suicide letter, it was the ending of one chapter and the beginning of a new one- ME. This chapter of my life is where I rise from the ashes a better version of myself and go after everything that's mines! I waited patiently for this very moment. This is my season. I know my worth, and I've restored two of the most important things in my life, peace and happiness.

This time, I made a promise to myself to never lose Me again. I am willing let go of everything and everyone around me that is hurting or hindering me, before I let go of me. Once you get a good grip on yourself, hold on tight, and don't let go!

We have to be patient with ourselves. Some of the most beautiful success stories take time. I told you that I started working on this book four years ago. I would get so frustrated with myself for not completing it, but I had to realize that my story was still being written. I had not yet lived through the moments that this book consists of. My story was not done, and it still isn't.

Our journey is never truly finished - we continue living, learning, and growing. I can definitely say that I am not the same woman four years ago that I am today. I needed to mature in my journey and be strong enough to withstand the things that had broken me in the past.

I doubted myself for years. I was so accustomed to not finishing anything that I would allow those negative thoughts to get the best of me. I was the one thing that was standing between me and my purpose by holding on to my past and all of the things that were hindering me.

Maybe it's time you to set flames to the things in your life that have been keeping you from reaching your full potential. Although this isn't a "self-help" book or some expert guide on how to heal or live your life, I do hope that by sharing my story, that I have inspired you to take the necessary steps to overcome your biggest enemy - SELF. And after you too have mastered the art of healing, I hope that you too share your stories with others because your story could save somebody's life.

Chapter 10
Here

Here is where your Healing starts…

About Diosha Davis

Diosha Davis is a mother, an Army Veteran and has worked in the hospital as an Environmental Care Manager for several years. Diosha was born and raised in Dallas, Texas and moved to Houston in 2017. In her first published book, "Healing Starts Here", Diosha shares her past; revealing truths about her encounters with life threatening circumstances, addictions, trials, and setbacks. She expresses why self-Love and vulnerability are so important to healing. She is an impeccable example of what it truly means to overcome and an amazing representation of RESILIENCE. Diosha has always had a passion for mentoring and caring for others, even during some of the darkest times in her life. "No one can make you feel inadequate about the things you've learned to accept, love, and appreciate about yourself. So, don't just walk in your Truth, you have to STRUT in it!"

Connect with Diosha www.dioshadavis.com

www.ingramcontent.com/pod-product-compliance
Lightning Source LLC
Chambersburg PA
CBHW021242090426
42740CB00006B/651